America, Our Children,

Ourselves

A Quest for Insight/Action

By

Naomi A. Brookins

ISBN: 1-4033-3378-5 (e-book)
ISBN: 1-4033-3379-3 (Paperback)
ISBN: 1-4033-3380-7 (Dustjacket)

This book is printed on acid free paper.

1st Books - rev. 9/4/02

ACKNOWLEDGEMENT

This book is dedicated to the memory of my first Principal, Mrs. Ernestine Curry of Oliver Wendell Holmes Elementary School and all of the students who touched my life. It also acknowledges the joys of working with those students who were members of my Great Books Program. All of them were outstanding in their ability to think reflectively as we discussed many outstanding readings.

This writing is also dedicated to the memories of George Washington High School students and to my college students in the subject of Learning Resources.

It's just great to know that our lives merged; thereby, creating a setting for excellent teaching, learning, and application.

Naomi A. Brookins

Chicago, Illinois

May 2002

INTRODUCTION

Today, as we rightfully soar upward and surge ahead within our dynamic, uncompromising technological 21st century, our educational system demands that we accept the uncompromising responsibility of forever transforming the lives of teachers and students.

"America, our Children, Ourselves" addresses the many concerns of our educational system in crisis. This message is a universal cry for insight/action.

Throughout my tenure as an educator, I've taught at the elementary and high school levels. I've lectured at the college level in the subject of Learning Resources in Education and curriculum. At the same time, I became extensively involved with the study of the educational process. Therefore, this study is an insightful conclusion as to where we are today, and how we must move ahead with hope, power, and action.

I found that my fundamental concerns were the relationship between education in its broadest scope and the dimension of living experiences that give value, meaning, wholeness and purpose to life. I also found that our time-tested virtues had been removed from the process and places on reserve.

It is now time for dads and moms to-be to re-visits the quality of their lives before conception. They need to know, without a doubt, that they have the power — because of the standard of taste that they have chosen for themselves — to empower their children by giving them a healthy physical, mental, and spiritual head start for life. They owe this to themselves, their children, and our world.

As parents begin to integrate their children into their family structure, a new ethic of commitment must help to preserve certain older values that Americans cherish. At the same time, however, they must safeguard new one that they are integrating into their personal family structure.

Researchers in the study of Child Development have proven that from birth to three years of age lay the foundation for future learning. They believe that this is the time when young children experience the joy of being loved, and the comfort and consolation of family life.

Because of this bonding in the family — and as your child becomes older — he or she will begin to understand a healthy family structure. He or she will begin to enjoy the freedom of a secure well being. When this is achieved, a more caring attitude will become evident. Then the appreciation for the awe, mysteries and sacredness of live will come into focus.

When families have become empowered with a delicate standard of taste that is uncompromising, the members are ready to join other families and begin to establish church families. All will become teachers and learners in the process of educating.

Schools and communities are recipients of many kinds of families. It is at this time when parents, principals, teachers, school counselors, students, and other community organizations began the awesome task of preparing all for learning and living.

Today, more than ever before in our history, we must take an in-depth look for the reasons why too many of our elementary and high school students are falling through the cracks of our educational system.

For example, beginning in the year 1996 and in one of our southern states, violence erupted in a school shooting. More and more school shooting occurred across our nation. They continue until this day. It seems to be an epidemic of violence.

I believe that today we have a lost generation who is looking for identity. Their cries are resounding loud and clear across our country. Have they truly gotten our attention?

As we develop insight that will bring about positive action into the declining character of our youth, we must never forget that they are the ones who will keep our country healthy and alive.

Even though the 16th President of America had the awesome responsibility of preserving the Union and ending slavery during the United States Civil War, he took time to remind the American People about the future of our country, our children/ourselves.

AND MAY WE BE REMINDED... It has been recorded that Abraham Lincoln said, "A child is a person who is going to carry on what you have started. He is going to sit where you are sitting, and when you are gone, attend to those things you think are important. You many adopt all of the policies you please, but how they are carried out depends on him. He will assume control of your cities, states, and nations. He is going to move in and take over your churches, schools, universities, and corporations ... the fate of humanity is in his hands."

Abraham Lincoln

CONTENTS

Chapter 1

EVEN BEFORE CONCEPTION, PLAN TO GIVE YOUR FUTURE BABY A HEALTHY HEAD START FOR LIFE

Dads and moms to-be, please accept this fact as being your greatest ever. Without a doubt, you have embedded within all that you are the greatest possibility, the greatest responsibility, and the greatest satisfaction of helping to shape the life of your future children, even before conception. This is a true and time-tested statement and its validity has been proven over and over again.

Within your inborn power that envelopes all that you are lies these two factors; namely, common sense and your delicate standard of taste that creates a healthy life for abundant living. When these two factors are not omitted from your creative thinking, you have the power to make the right tough choices for your style of living. These right choices will lead to creative thinking/action that will take you away from the unreal world of depravity and moral decay that is eating away at the nucleus of our society.

Therefore, then and only then, will both of you be able to experience a healthy self-fulfillment by knowing that you have cooperated with the natural purity of conception. Your cooperation has helped to lay the foundation for a healthy start for your embryo.

Now that I've gotten your attention, I hope that we can move ahead through many interactive stages of causes and effects. I have opened the door for your reflective thinking and analysis. As you pass through this reflective stage, I hope that you will enter the subjective and then the objective stages of critical thinking/action.

Shall we take a brief look at the heredity and environmental factors that you have preserved for your child even before birth.

With the mechanisms of heredity and environment in mind, I believe that both of these — or you might feel comfortable with these words nature and nurture — jointly fashion a person's abilities, skills, and psychological characteristics. I don't believe that we can clearly determine which one of these is more influential. We can, however, state that they function within an interlocking/interactive process that determines certain all-important characteristics of the whole person.

Throughout the study of human development, we find that genes control the development of tissues and organs of the body, and hence the way in which it functions. These functions clearly affect behavior for such organs as the brain, the senses, and muscles.

Within this setting, we clearly see the case for many complex and psychologically characteristics such as intelligence, temperament, and aptitude. These, too, depend so very much on heredity.

Now, moms and dads, to be able to comprehend all of these dynamic statements with all of their ramifications, you must allow yourself to become an introverted thinker who is deeply in touch with one's self. You must listen to the reflective side of yourself. And more importantly, you must become totally aware as to whether you want your child to live up to his/her greatest genetic potential.

In our quest for more information in human development, we find that the genetic potential begins when the male and female come together and form DNA., the genetic endowment that determines a person's physical and mental characteristics. Biologically speaking, this is because the embryo from fertilization is alive, human, complete and growing. Therefore, what both of you have brought to this conceptual reality have created the quality of the inner world, the womb, in which your baby will live and develop for the next nine month.

What great joy and responsibility to know that both moms and dads are the first human beings to touch and influence the life of their embryo.

Never forget that you have already determined whether he or she will, from the moment of conception, begin to develop a powerful genetic potential for life. Remember that because both of your bodies were free of all transmittable diseases and drugs, the complex building blocks of nature are free to

do their job. Now is the time when we truly

have something great to CELEBRATE.

Chapter 2

DADS AND MOMS AS TOWERS OF STRENGTH, UNDERSTANDING, AND PEACE

During the nine months in which bonding, development, and growth are taking place within the uterus, dads and moms must vigorously seek and develop strength and understanding for all that is taking place within their lives. They must also become outstanding guardians of peace. These attributes are crucial for all as the fetus begins its journey of preparing to enter the outer world.

The bonding, development and growth can become an unbreakable chain of love that will bind both of you closer together for each day, and even the many tomorrows.

Within this complex state of physical and mental development, many changes are taking place within the mom's body. All of these changes will affect the development of the fetus. For example, as communication begins to take place between the mom and fetus, the feeling of stress or peace that mom might experience is passed on to the fetus. Therefore, the amount of emotional excitement could affect normal development.

Moms and dads, remember that researches have found that even before birth, babies learn how physical objects behave by moving their body parts. Therefore, moms must be prepared to experience much physical action from the fetus. For example, a sucking sensation, kicking, the forming of round solid state, and much more physical action can take place.

These positions can become very uncomfortable. However, a gentle touch/movement of the stomach with the hand will communicate love and a more comfortable feeling for both mom and fetus.

In addition to asking your Pediatrician for information on prenatal care, there are priceless information located in colleges, universities, public libraries and the Internet/Web sites.

The following are just a few of the questions that you might want answered:

1. What is taking place in the development of the embryo at 6-8 weeks/56 days?

2. How many weeks will it be before I experience movement within my uterus?

3. How many months will it take before this movement/action increases?

4. At the seventh month, what stage of development will the fetus have reached?

5. At the beginning of birth, what role will the fetus play as labor pains begin?

After your baby has aggressively propelled itself from the world of darkness of the womb into the outer world, don't be afraid to feel good about yourselves. It is time to celebrate this moment with much joy. As your baby's loud cry resounds across the delivery room, rejoice.

It is now time to remember that you — even before conception — were not afraid to allow yourselves/action to become awakened to the great challenge. You allowed the purity and natural characteristics to come together and create a healthy foresight, strength and will.

15

You became a healthy factor in the conceptual process.

Again, I say "REJOICE."

Chapter 3

INTEGRATING YOUR BABY INTO

YOUR

FAMILY STRUCTURE

Even as early as the 4th Century B.C., Western thinkers have not been able to define the family as a never changing institution. Nevertheless, they all agree that the family is the center for our ever expanding world. They also agree that the family's nucleus must contain many visible and invisible ingredients that will empower its members for society's complex circle of living.

To create a system of character building in your home, requires the ability for you to make many tough choices. Always remember, however, that you're a free moral agent. This is to say that you have the responsibility and right to make choices for yourself and your family.

As you begin to establish the depth, height, and scope of your choices in relation to your family and our society, you will have accepted a hard-won humility relating to the welfare of our nation. This hard-won humility gives you a giant spiritual step forward toward a deeper sense of humaneness.

Today, we seem to be living in a valueless society. It is the kind of society in which the moral fabric has eroded.

Therefore, we must, within our personal families develop a system of values by which to measure all that we are.

These personal values must be strong enough to combat the many depraved social signals that communicate confusion to our global society. It is the kind of confusion that weakens the ability of the young to make the right tough choices for their lives. This confusion also leads to disarray in the home, church, school and community.

If the ability to make the right tough choices does not begin in the home/family, all of our institutions will inherit many, many kinds of faltering standards of taste. These faltering standards of taste will develop into faltering leadership characteristics that will display irresponsible thinking and action. This will lead to disarray in the highest office in our land, and its effects will be felt around the world.

Within the 21st Century and within the Western world, we must return to the time-tested facts that the family/home is the institution where action learning takes place within an established curriculum before the school years. Your family structure, therefore, must become a powerful continuous process of structuring and empowerment for the good of all members.

In spite of the dismal state of our society, you must lay the foundation for your family to develop a living standard of taste which cannot be intimidated. This delicacy of structuring must contain the elements of social health, action and strength. All of these are necessary as your family leads the way in taking the many critical steps of renewing an uncompromising social ethics of commitment for our world.

Now that your structuring is insightfully progressing, you're ready to integrate your baby into your family structure.

Educators from many walks of life have done extensive research in the subject of

Human Development. They have given us an extraordinary new understanding of the child from birth to three years of age.

We now know that from birth to three years are very important developmental years in the life of a child. These early experiences will affect your child's later ability to learn and reason.

Therefore, the child must be enveloped with love by the parents' nurturing care. The child must be taught human goodness, well being, love, responsibility, and trust. All of these wonderful characteristics that are taught, must

23

be embedded in daily living by all in the family.

These early experiences will lay the foundation for later understanding the Golden Rule; namely,

Confucianism

What you don't want done to yourself, don't do to others—SIXTH CENTURY, B.C.

Buddhism

Hurt not others with that which pains thyself—FIFTH CENTURY, B.C.

Jainism

In happiness and suffering, in joy and grief, we should regard all creatures as we regard our own self, and should therefore refrain from inflicting upon others such injury as would appear undesirable to us if inflicted upon ourselves—FIFTH CENTURY, B.C.

Classical Paganism

May I do to others as I would that they would do unto me—Plato-FOURTH CENTURY, B.C.

Judaism

What is hateful to yourself, don't do to your fellow man—Rabbi Hillel—FIRST CENTURY, B.C.

Christianity

Whatsoever ye would that men should do to you, do ye even so to them—Jesus of Nazareth-FIRST CENTURY, A.D.

Sikhism

Treat others as thou wouldst be treated thyself-SIXTEENTH CENTURY, A.D.

Therefore, what the family is surrounded with in the home, will determine the outcome of all of its members. With this kind of environment in the home, your baby, older children, teenagers, and adults will have a healthy and powerful environment to live in and practice love and respect for all. They will continue to grow into wholeness of person and purpose.

At this point in my writing I've only referred to dads and moms to-be from our society's traditional family setting. However, I must emphatically now state that this message is also intended for dads and moms who are single parents.

You as single parents must have the same vision for your family. Your insight into the quality of life for all in the family must light a vista of hope and empowered action from before birth and continue throughout all of our societies' institutions. Therefore, your job at all times will require action that is representative for both single dads and moms.

In a report written as early as 1979, various statistics support the thesis that children from one-parent families are a growing minority.

Therefore, you must always be aware and not allow your child to be pushed into divided loyalties and grow into feeling alienated from the "real family" model.

Therefore, what the family is surrounded by in the home will determine the outcome of its members. With this kind of love and action surroundings in the home, your baby, older children, teenagers, and adults will have created a healthy and powerful environment to live in and practice love and respect for all. All of the family members will continue to grow into wholeness of person/purpose as all members venture our into the larger world and

all of its institutions.

   Are you ready to move on?

Chapter 4

CHURCHES ILLUMINATE VISTAS

OF

FAITH/ACTION FOR ALL PEOPLE

Churches are one of the most important and powerful institutions in our society. They, too, can be defined as the priceless and needed curriculum before the school years, during the school years, and beyond the school years. They are where people gather and become empowered in faith/action. This faith/action becomes cemented in the hearts and lives of children, teenagers, adults, and even extended families. Without a doubt, churches are absolutely necessary for the improvement of our society.

When the scope of the curriculum of the church is expanded to meet the needs of all members and non-members, the teaching, learning, and living process has begun to develop. This process culminates in developing a system of personal values against which the lives of its members can be measured. This is the continuing process of the growth of the human spirit.

The members and non-members are not afraid of loosing their individuality, but rather gaining it. This is accomplished when each person evaluates his or her thoughts and ideas for the good of all. Socrates once stated that "humankind must know themselves."

Throughout the ages and even today, all kinds of families from all walks of life come together to establish churches. Some of the families have been given a head start within their home. They have developed a standard of taste for living abundantly. This delicacy of taste empowers then to love God, their neighbor, and themselves. The members of this kind of family are able to convey their finest emotions for living. Their lives also demonstrate lives of strength, hope, a healthy self-fulfillment, decision making ability, and they are always opened to listening and sharing with others.

Therefore, when these kinds of families come into the churches, they are spiritually equipped to explain why one must turn away from all principles that may not lead to a wholesome end.

There are also many families who are defined as dysfunctional. Their families have found it very difficult to even begin to develop wholeness for both children and adults. They, too, are a necessary and vital part of this institution, the church.

We must never forget that the dysfunctional families come seeking self-fulfillment, identity, refinement of life, and acceptance within the whole church family. They are elated about acquiring information for their lives. They are also ready to develop a standard of taste which will allow them to transcend the negative parts of their thinking and living. They are very eager to develop power and faith in action for their lives.

We must never forget the single-parent families who come to churches. Members must always be equipped to minister to these families. If the families have just gone through the process of "falling apart", members must be sensitive to the trauma experienced by both parents and children.

This is the time when the church members must provide a structured setting in the life of both parents and children. You see, this may be a time when the major structure of life seems to be crumbling.

Children who have been labeled "Children Of the Ghetto" will become part of our churches. They, too, may be struggling with moral dilemma. They may not have developed a clear cut form of moral logic or reasoning to help them to decide which way shall I go with my life.

We must never forget that the self-fulfillment search which begins to take place in the home must be continued in the churches and all other institutions in our society. This search is a more complex, fateful, and irreversible phenomenon than simply the by product of affluence of a shift in the national character toward narcissism. Today, it is truly the search for a new American philosophy of life that is desperately needed in today's world, the 21st Century.

At this time in the life of the congregation, the members should not be concerned with abstract historic issues. The arena in which all struggle is the everyday life. This specifically can be called the "giving getting complex" - the unwritten rules that governing what we get in marriage, work, school, community, and sacrifices for others, and what are the things others expect in return.

These unwritten rules are so very vital to the American life. When we launch out on this cultural revolution, the upheavals we encounter in the giving/getting compact are among the principal signs of the arrival.

Never forget that this is the time when leaders of churches and families become learners and teachers. As all people reach for goal of self-fulfillment that will empower them to live more abundantly, all should be able to transmit meaning for their lives and discuss the values that they have found essential for their own self-fulfillment.

In addition to family and non-family groups coming to churches, many members go out into communities and reach and touch the lives of many. As they go, they become an anchor for the bereaved, the unhappy, the unloved, the suffering, and the many homeless and older citizens.

These groups help parents in the communities, as well as churches, to minister to the needs of the young. They are also able to bring dignity and meaning for living to the lowest existence.

Under an umbrella of love and teaching, churches help the individual to continually re-assess the meaning and values that are transmitted from one person to the other. Within this kind of gathering, there will be perspective and thought provoking members.

These members help others to abandon insufficient notions about a healthy self-fulfillment.

Therefore, with all of this faith and action living demonstrated in the lives of church members, they are preparing to light a few torches here and there in schools, communities, and campuses around the world. This power will continue to bring about a spiritual revolution that will change the world. We must remember that as this is being done, we're using time-tested solution that are bringing hope to humanity.

Chapter 5

SCHOOLS AND COMMUNITIES

Schools and communities are recipients of both home and church families. Both of these institution become assimilated into the structuring process of schools and communities. Principals, teachers, school counselors, student, parents and community groups are vital catalysis within the educational circle of learning.

If America is to continue to be the leader of the free world in the 21st century, it is absolutely necessary that all of its citizens understand that these four institutions; namely, the home, church families, schools and communities are so interwoven, so interdependent to the extent that each must know that it cannot function in isolation of the other. Togetherness establishes a foundation for excellent teacher and learning. This kind of quality teaching and learning leads to wholeness of purpose/person.

Beginning with the family in the home, parents must regain control over their children and continue to work with the institutions they support to teach their offspring.

All of our institutions must prove to themselves and others that they are aggressive partners within the educational circle of learning. This becomes evident as each group reaches out to the other and asks for help.

With this kind of quality and quantity of communication shared by all, a greater understanding and appreciation of diverse cultures and ideas come into focus. This leads to a special linkage of power that will cement a climate for teaching and learning.

Now that the home, churches, schools and communities have reached out and found a linkage that will benefit all, they must now reach out to the many youth serving agencies; namely, the recreational agencies, the institutions of higher education, the libraries and librarians, civic groups, and many other groups and persons. All of the youth serving agencies must be allowed to feel that they, too, are very important educators and learners.

Where are we today with education in our technological world? Are we bold enough to take an in-depth look at the state of too many of our institutions? I believe that if we're surge ahead with education for our youth, we have no other choice but to be bold.

Without a doubt, too many of our institutions are in disarray. Too many do not accept virtue as necessary for educating our youth. Many leaders of too many of our schools and communities become insulted when they are asked to accept social continuity from the home and church families.

Because of this rejection, a needed source of character and spiritual values have been placed on reserve.

As I take an in-depth look at the statistics of lost lives and abuses in the timeline of recent school shootings, I'm mentally forced to look at the landscape of our schools and communities from an ideologically point of view.

For example, from February 2, 1996 in Moses Lake, Washington through May 7, in Williamsport, Pennsylvania, too many of our students and teachers were killed or hurt in violent shootings in our schools. Today, make no mistake, this kind of violence have not altogether ceased.

These were some of the adolescents who became increasingly engaged in killing others and themselves, and hurting and abusing others and themselves. They allowed themselves to become enveloped into a abyss of drugs and nothingness.

Today, too many of our students are participating in many kinds of sexual activities that could lead to sexually transmitted diseases.

I hope that our youth now have the attention of the parents, churches, schools and communities. These young people's voices resounded and still are resounding across America and the world.

I believe that their cries were saying the following: Listen to me, I can't breathe, don't you care what happens to many of us? They seemed to be saying that they had no anchor for their lives. Please help me because I'm not able to accept the responsibility for my actions; I've lost my cool and I'm out of control. I'm going to take care of those who have isolated and bullied me.

We must never forget that the cries of our children were and still are loud and clear. Have we truly heard them? If we have, we must tenaciously hold on to the meaning of their cries. We must begin to make the many needed changes within our educational system.

When we — and we must — find the courage to do this, our youth will begin to create a watershed for a historic and even nobler theme of wholeness of person/purpose.

It is very, very important to remember that when it comes to communicating with those youth who might fall through the cracks of our society, not enough of our educators have the necessary skills.

Too many dads and moms have not taught their youth the principles of the Golden Rule. Therefore, these youth have not developed a standard of taste for quality of character and respect that honor themselves and others. Within this setting, they have not been taught right from wrong actions that are prized by American society at large.

Scholars from many disciplines agree that the most important factors in the success of students' lives must be implemented at the right time by each institution.

This is done as the student move from phase to phase in his growth and development.

Many of our leaders agree that in a complex society such as we have today, there is great and priceless wisdom in having allies and partners with whom risks can be shared. This kind of hard-won humility becomes a giant step toward a sense of humanity. This humanity is centered in the educational circle of learning.

When our forefathers came to America, they brought with them time-honored ways of schooling. These time-honored ways included traditions handed down by the Hebrew, Greek, and Roman people. Today, in many of our institutions, these time-honored traditions are working for many people, including those who were excluded from the educational process at the time of its establishment.

Our government, other leaders of our nation, and the American people accepted these time-honored ways. They now know, more than ever before, that if we're to educate the whole person, moral and spiritual values are indispensable in this process. They were aware, just as we are today, of the delicate line that separates church and state.

Today, more than ever before and because of too much depravity within America' society and societies around the world, the average citizen accepts the visual fact that moral and spiritual values are absolutely necessary for educating the whole person. They accept the basic functions of education as the basic functions of humanity.

These functions are intellectual, moral, spiritual, social, economics, political, physical, domestic, aesthetics, and recreational. However, the other needed function that demands to be added today is "ideology." If ideology is not included, all others become null and void within the kind of technological world that we live in today. Therefore, the survival of our civilization demands that we look at the world and ourselves in imperialistic terms as well as moralistic terms.

This kind of thinking, teaching, and learning call for restructuring our thinking and living to meet the needs of an ever changing world.

All of the basic functions are part of the aspects of the whole person; although, in a separable way, they are organically related like the organs of the body. This is say that all of the functions act interdependently to bring about wholeness of person/purpose for living.

We who are reaching and touching the lives of all kinds of people throughout the world must ask ourselves the following questions:

What is education?

Who or what is to be educated?

Is it a person or just a technological machine?

Does it or he or she have a physical body and an inner self?

If we conclude that it is a person who has both a physical body and an inner self, we're now ready to prepare a whole person for life.

Education, then, can be defined as the process of preparing a person for life.

All of our students must be able to accept the fact that life is practical. Education must be practical and usable. Everyone must learn to work, must earn his keep; and must do it in the best and happiest way possible.

Students must learn that life is very dynamic. Education must be vital, alive, and active. Life must empower a person to join a world that is soaring upward and surging ahead. Life is recreational and friendly. Education teaches the art of living with people of all races, colors, and creeds. Life is cooperative. This is to say that each person has a place in his or her community. There are duties to be performed by everyone as we begin to feel that we truly are members of a group. We then begin to believe that we are truly our brother's "keeper."

Education must also be many living experiences. Through these experiences, the person discovers that his richest opportunities are within his reach. The person must be insightful enough to expand his or her own outlook for living. The person must be creative enough to build a place as a citizen within society. The person must be subjective enough to increase the fragrance of his own nature. He or she must be knowledgeable enough to know that all these powerful and priceless elements are found through ceaseless cooperation with others.

We as teachers and learners must never forget that all of the youth whom we reach and touch are soaring upward and surging ahead within their own personal world of imagination, hope, ideals, and dreams. And for us to be able to provide those youth with a

61

stake of the greatest dreams and ideals is quite a task. This task demands that we light a vista of hope/empowered action for today and their future.

We know that a productive life demands that we discuss our ideologies and listen to the ideologies of others at home and throughout the world. As we take a revisionist look at our own hopes, our aspirations, defeats, and triumphs of the past, we give those whose lives we continue to touch the living reality for their lives. These, to me, are some of the greatest aims of education.

Therefore, when all of these empowered characteristics are inducted into the thinking and action of our youth, we will then be able to measure their growth and achievements — not by their ability to pass a verbal examination — but by their readiness to face and solve problems within their lives. Then, and only then, will their pet-up energies not break out into violent rebellion or escape into neurotic fantasies.

Chapter 6

INTEGRATING INSIGHT, HOPE/ACTION INTO OUR DYNAMIC TECHNOLOGICAL 21ST CENTURY

As we rightfully soar upward and surge ahead within the 21st century, we must do so with thinking and action that comes from reviewing, cultivating, and restructuring a delicate part of our ideology for America and the world.

Without a doubt, we truly are the leading free nation of the world. This statement demands a re-thinking and re-administering many of our sociopolitical programs at home and abroad. It is also true that our educational system at home and abroad demands this kind of action.

We must never, never forget that a nation cannot remain free and illiterate at the same time. Parents must regain control over their children and interact with the institutions they support to teach their offspring.

Therefore, all of our institutions must abolish all needless educational filibustering, all educational hedging, and all educational indecisiveness. These negative and outdated characteristics have no place within a progressive system of education.

As we pass the torch of liberty and freedom to the next generation, we must have already taken a revisionist look at our time-tested ways of dealing with people at home and around the world.

This time around, however, we must not allow ourselves to remain hypocritical when it comes to the added basic function in ideology and action.

For example, Jefferson's 2nd paragraph in the Declaration of Independence proposed a condensed statement of the natural law-compact philosophy then prevalent in America.

This great document says, "We hold these truths to be self-evident, that all men are created equal, that they are endowed by their Creator with certain unalienable rights, that among these are life, liberty, and the pursuit of happiness. That to secure these rights, governments are instituted among men, deriving their just powers from the consent of the governed…"

Because of the powerful message of this document, the Declaration of Independence of July 4, 1776, we must bring to the table thinking and action of inclusiveness for all people. This includes those whose ancestors were brought to America in chains and those Native Americans who were already here.

If we're to make these ideas workable for all people, we must be able to accept the fact that we sometimes forced on our people and other nations and their people too much verbiage with little action.

Even though the Negroes who were forcefully bound, welded together, and forced to come to America, they were then made to feel that they were strangers in their own land. However, there were those who gave their lives for freedom, and others who somehow managed to work out many great messages that they had for humanity.

69

Because of so many injustices inflicted upon the Negroes, too many never became aware of their identity. Today, however, until America accepts Negro Americans as equals who have assimilated themselves into the greatness of our society, America, too, will not know her identity.

We Americans must never forget that our country is not a nations of individuals. It is a "nations of nations." Black Americans, therefore, must pursue their rights not as individuals, but as a member of a black race whose cultural has influenced the entire

American cultural scene. We must never forget that the Negro, too, is America and that his presence must be felt.

America must represent all of its people. This 21st century is the time to begin. All nationalities must take their places within the whole society. In this way, and through a dynamic kind of "internal imperialism," all people will be able to take on the business that must be done.

In an effort to move forward with more insight and action, we must take a more comprehensive look at America and the world at the time of the establishment of our system. We know that in the 1940s, our idealistic ways of dealing with nations have not always been successful.

It is obvious that if nations of the world are to be able to induct peace into the landscape of our world, all must accept the fact that the continuous struggle for existence is fundamental and will forever be the nature of things.

Therefore, as we continue to use insight/action for ourselves and the world, we must listen to the voices of wisdom, common sense, judgment, and diplomacy at home and around the world. We already know that when the stakes of life call for very practical judgment, the criteria are always relative. We must always be prepared to hit a home run. This, because we know that there is no such thing as "absolute power" for any nation.

Do you remember that it was in the 1940s when our guidelines for avoiding wars, preparing for wars, and settling them were not comprehensive enough? Because of this, today we ask the question "Why are we having so many problems with ourselves and other nations as we struggle to agree on so many very important matters?

We know that the presence of rivalry, conflict, and strife will always be evident among nations, states, and communities. This is the normal condition of humanity.

Let us never forget, therefore, that we must always remain powerful enough to promote and protect Democratic principles around the world. Many of these principles are under assault. We must continue to arrest the present trends of convergence of rising international decisions, and the codes that will undo the international codes of conduct that foster the peaceful resolutions of disputes between nations. Within this setting, we see many symptoms that will never work in a free society.

These symptoms are terrorism, subversion, and conquest that are already seeking to destroy the democratic way of life. We must never forget that the ideals and safety of democratic societies around the world are under assault.

Chapter 7

EDUCATING FOR THE 9/11/2001

CHANGED

LANDSCAPE IN AMERICA AND

THE WORLD

As I began to gather my writings and research materials for this book in early 2001, I never would have believed that the peaceful, ideological, and sociopolitical landscape of

America and the world would become what it is today.

Even in 1995 when I traveled to Oklahoma City, Oklahoma to give support to friends who were emotionally torn apart because of the terrorist act that destroyed the Alfred P Murrah Federal Building, I comforted myself by believing that terrorism rarely happened in America. I became less afraid when this was proven that the terrorists were not the work of international terrorism, but of a self-described patriot named Timothy McVeigh, a U.S. Army veteran and right-wing antigovernment extremist. His terrorist act killed more than 168 people.

On August 7, 1998 when car bombs exploded outside of two United States embassies in two African Capitals, Nairobi and Dar es Salaam killing more than 224 people, I still convinced myself that this happened on another continent, and could never, never happen on American' soil.

Because I'm a very concerned American citizen and an American History teacher, I knew that terrorists had been striking at American targets around the world since 1993.

However, today, 2002, the unthinkable has become a reality. The American people now know that the Complex Web of terrorism is America's new and greatest enemy.

America and the world know that on September 11, 2001, the peaceful, ideological, and sociopolitical landscape of America and the world changes forever.

Until a few minutes beyond 8:00 a.m. on this day, anyone who enjoyed looking at the two towers of the World Trade Center would have said that they looked so very beautiful and stately as they towered over 16 acres of land.

Now the UNTHINKABLE happened. Before 9:00 a.m. on September 11, 2001 in New York City, New York, an American Airline Flight II, a Boeing 767, slammed into the north tower of the World Trade Center.

Less than two hours later, the twin 110—story skyscraper collapsed and plunged into an abyss of nothingness. It was at this very moment when I became so very concerned about all of those people who worked in that 16 acres complex. I later recalled that more than 80 countries of the world were represented by thousands of people.

I then began to wonder if those who sat adjacent to each other and also those who worked with others throughout the towers, had ever taken the opportunity to get to know one another by exchanging ideas. I asked myself this question: Had any of those people taken the opportunity to talk about how nations and people should live together in such a complex world as ours?

My thinking was interrupted by another UNTHINKABLE attack when another hijacked American Airline Boeing 757 out of Dulles International Airport in Herndon, Virginia plowed into the Pentagon, the headquarters for the United States Department of Defense just outside of our nation's capital.

The nightmare continues as a United Airline Flight 93 had been hijacked with the intention of crashing into the White House or Capitol building. Even though I became very disturbed about all of the people on that plane, it was very good to know that they had the courage to force the plane down into a field in Pennsylvania.

When these terrorist attacks were over, the abyss of destruction and nothingness had become a 16 acre valley of death — and yes, hope.

As I continued to watch the horror unfold on television, I remembered and accepted the comforting words of the 23rd Psalms, "Even though I walk through the valley of the shadow of death, I will fear no evil, for you, GOD, are with me." —Psalms 24:4.

After the great helplessness had escaped from the inner turmoil that was taking place in the lives of Americans and people around the world, people from all walks of life gathered at ground zero and became their brother's and sister's keepers. When the statistics were compiled they showed that over 5,000.00 people including 300.00 firemen and 40.00 policemen lost their lives.

Yes, we all know that our wide, wide global world has become so very small. It has also become more and more complicated. Therefore, if any of the nations of the world are to survive, all nations must function interdependently.

We saw the act of interdependency working through the spirit of faith and action across America and the world. All people allowed their courage to become the struggle for justice and peace.

Therefore, when it seems to be prudent for our leaders to make bold statements of courage and strength, it just might be better to look at the complete landscape of the world.

Even today in the month of April 2002 and as I attempt to conclude this writing, I cannot believe that the citizens of the world have accepted — and will ever be able to accept — or completely comprehend the great magnitude of these terrorist attacks.

As for me, I know that there will never be the feeling of absolute security, comfort, and peace in our ever changing and complex world.

However, as we continue day by day to fight the enemy of fear within and the enemy of fear without, my thoughts began to focus on our homes, churches, schools, communities, governments, and the many organizations at home and around the world.

My question now is, what do we really say to our youth who must govern our world?

First of all, as we continue to reach, touch, and help them to find the purpose for themselves and the world, we must always remind them that they are the future and the fate of humanity is in their hands.

As we, their teachers and friends, fade into the background of our ever changing society and continue to support freedom of living for all, we're passing the torch of life, liberty, and the pursuit of happiness on to them. We must let them know that we have authorized them to accept the responsibility of always keeping the democratic way of life alive.

To keep the democratic way of life alive and working, all must continue to cultivate the ability to explain why democracy works for America and people around the world. All of our youth must continue to develop listening skills that will enable communication to occur between people of all nations.

This preceding statement can be thought as the process of shared inquiry. It is within the process where all of the participants accept the responsibility of mapping out the territory in which discussions of ideas should take place. If this kind of communication is not demonstrated in the thinking, the lives, and actions of our youth, all efforts for a peaceful solution will become stagnated.

For example, the ability to bring about peace in the Mideast will never be accomplished until the leaders of the Palestinian and Israeli people began to listen to each other.

These leaders must begin to use the method of shared inquiry. This kind of communication will allow all of those who are at the table to listen and comprehend all of the ideas that are shared. They will then be able to ask questions of the evaluative nature.

Therefore, if these kinds of questions are to bring about answers that will light vistas for solving some of the many problems of these two countries and the world, all participants must be able to think factually, subjectively, and objectively. They must also be able to defend the outcome of their thinking.

As our youth continue to move ahead by utilizing the empowerment of courage, they do so with faith and resolve intertwined in a very tight rope. Their ideas and their body language will say to the American people and the world that they, with all that is within them, truly believe in their creator. This action/statement will also speak to their parents, churches, teachers, schools and communities. This is because our youth believe that victory will come as they struggle for a better world.

All people of the world know that the struggle will be long and will seem like an eternity. However, we must all know that this is what has to be done if the world is to become a dynamic world that represents people of all nations.

And now, I'm saying to our youth. At the end of your days and years when you need more time to reflect on the purpose of your struggles, I've compiled a list of quotes on pages 93-96 for your reflection.

TIMELESS QUOTES:

My days, my hopes, and yes my life had taken on a new dimension. My faith in GOD and in myself had lit a vista for my life. —Brookins, Naom A., teacher, librarian, lecturer, educator, and author of "Naomi's Story: You Don't Have To Be Broken."

Common sense in an uncommon degree, is what the world calls wisdom. —Coleridge, Samuel Taylor, English poet, essays, and literary critic.

I will not be satisfied living my own life simply for myself. Other issues are more broader than my own little world. —Hill, Anita, Attorney.

The GREAT THING in the world is not so much where we stand, as in what direction we're moving. —Holmes, Oliver Wendell, American Author, and man of letters.

All that we send into the lives of others will come back into our own. —Kipling, Rudyard, English poet, novelist, and short-story writer.

Justice and truth are the common ties of society. —Locke, John, English philosopher.

Each one of us must earn our own existence. And how does anyone earn anything? Through perseverance, hard work, and desire. —Marshall, Thurgood, United States Supreme Justice.

We are the children of those who chose to survive. —From Daughter of the Dust by Nana Pouissant.

Every small positive change we can make in ourselves, repays in confidence in the future.

—Walker, Alice, Pulitzer Prize winning author.

ABOUT THE AUTHOR

Naomi A. Brookins is a long time resident of the Chatham Community located on the southeast side of the city of Chicago. She is an Elementary school teacher, a U.S. History teacher, a library/media specialist, a college lecturer, and a public speaker. She is an adult and teenage Bible teacher, an assistant superintendent of her church school, has created and directed many Easter, Christian, and heritage plays. She has also helped to establish a Christian Board of Education in her church and another church. She has established a church library in two other churches and worked extensively with missions. Naomi is the president of her community block club and continues to work with many churches and community organizations within the community of Chatham.

Naomi holds an AA degree, BA degree in Education, an MS degree in library science, an

MA in U.S. History, and did post graduate work at Northern Illinois University.

Naomi is also a recipient of the Superior Serve Award for her work in the Chicago Metropolitan Area, a recipient of the Outstanding Community Resident Award for her time and effort of dedication to the 6th Ward Community; was director of Region 3 of Illinois Association for Media in Education, and since 1991 has been a Docent at Harold Washington Library Center.

She spent twenty-five years of teaching for the Chicago Board of Education. There she touched the lives of many by leading then into thinking factually, subjectively, and reflectively about their vision for their lives, many subjects, and the world. She is also the proud mother of 4 sons.

Naomi is now the published author of *Naomi's Story: You Don't Have To Be Broken*, and *Youth Soaring Toward the Year 2001 By Making the Right Tough Choices Today*. Her latest book waiting to be published is titled, *America, Our Children, Ourselves: A Quest for Insight/Action.*

www.ingramcontent.com/pod-product-compliance
Lightning Source LLC
Chambersburg PA
CBHW051447280526
45785CB00003B/1466